THE ILLUSTRATED
TEXAS
DICTIONARY
of the
ENGLISH LANGUAGE
VOLUME FOUR

by Jim Everhart

with 47 photographs of the author
by Joe Shields

CLIFFS NOTES, INC. • LINCOLN, NEBRASKA 68501

ISBN   0-8220-1480-7

Yewston — the largest city in Texas. "Heidi, ah'm Gem Everhart and ah'm from *Yewston*, Texas."

mess — to fail to hit, catch, receive, see, hear, etc. "How'd yew *mess* that?"

blow — under, beneath.
"Luck out *blow!*"

dare — beloved or loved.
"That woman is *dare* to
mah heart."

shore — confident, convinced, positive.
"Are yew *shore* about that?"

fail — to have a sensation
of something. "Ah can jes
fail it in mah bones."

damon — an evil spirit. "Ah thank that man is possessed bah a *damon*."

better — having a harsh, disagreeably acrid taste. "Boy, is that stuff ever *better!*"

caper — a person who assumes responsibility for another's behavior. "Ah ain't mah brother's *caper!*"

etch — to feel a peculiar tingling of the skin that causes a desire to scratch. "Mah arm has *etched* all day."

mansion — to refer to briefly, to speak of. "Ah'm glad to do it. Don't *mansion* it."

sane — present participle of "say." "Yore crazy! Yew don't know what yore *sane!*"

sot — view, glimpse, something worth seeing. "That's a *sot* for sore ahs."

blade — to lose blood.
"If yew cut yore fanger
it's gonna *blade*."

tar — a tall building or structure. "That man is a *tar* of strenth."

bless — utter joy or contentment. "She's so happy she's in a state of *bless*."

poultry — the art of rhythmical composition. "Ah thank Shakespeare wrote the best *poultry*."

paints — trousers. "She wears the *paints* in that family."

wand — to adjust a mechanism for operation by some turning or coiling process. "Son of a gun, ah forgot to *wand* mah watch again!"

sprang — a season of the year. "We had the shortest *sprang* this year that ah can member."

wend — air in natural motion along the earth's surface. "That was some beg *wend* we had today."

claps — to fall, cave in, or crumble suddenly. "Ah thank that house is bout ready to *claps*."

swan — the domestic hog. "Yew don't cast pearls before *swan!*"

hoed — to have or keep in the hand; to grasp. "Cape a good *hoed* on them reins!"

heir — a mistake. "Luck at that! He made a *heir* at second base."

walled — unrestrained violence; fury.
"When he dranks, he becomes a *walled* man."

raisin — a basis or cause for some belief, action, or fact. "Give me one good *raisin* ah shouldn't do that!"

keds — children. "Ah want to talk to yew *keds* a minute."

dot — limitation on the amount of foods a person eats for reducing weight. "That *dot* ain't done yew a bit of good has it?"

blank — to open and close the eyes rapidly.
"That sunshine makes me *blank*."

pint — a colored liquid applied as decorative coating to various surfaces. "Yew main to tell me yew paid four dollars for that quart of *pint?*"

fall — metal in the form of very thin sheets. "One of mah hobbies is collectin' tin*fall*."

braid — race, strain, group, sort, or kind. "A hardened criminal is a altogether different *braid* of human bean."

cot — a light frame covered with some thin material to be flown in the wind at the end of a string. "Ah must a run thirty minutes to get that dad gum *cot* in the air."

pace — a separate or limited portion or quantity of something. "Could ah have another *pace* of that cake, Maam?"

clothes — near. "Boy, that was a *clothes* call!"

spade — rapidity in moving. "Come on now. We gotta *spade* thangs up."

farm — a document with blank spaces to be filled in with particulars.
"May ah have a *farm* to fill in, please?"

deaf — dexterous, nimble, skillful, clever.
"He shore is *deaf* at jugglin'."

parson — a human being. "That there is the lass *parson* in the world ah wanted to see today."

Sunny — the day after Saturday.
"Did yew want me to teach
Sunny school again this year?"

trod — attempted, endeavored. "We *trod* everythang we could thank of to hep them folks."

sabra — horse-like African animal having a pattern of black and white stripes. "Mah favorite animal at the zoo is the *sabra*."

warm — any of numerous long, slender, soft-bodied, legless, bilateral invertebrates.
"One of these days the *warm* is gonna turn."

rapid — irrationally extreme in opinion or practice. "He's one of the most *rapid* baseball fans in the state."

destined — far off. "Aw, that ain't gonna happen til the *destined* future."